Write it right!

The Art of Captivating Storytelling!

ANNA KATMORE

WRITE IT RIGHT –

The Art of captivating Storytelling

Cover design: Anna Katmore

www.annakatmore.com

Table of contents

Dear Writer

Forewords often get skipped, but if you're still here, let me make it worth your time.

First, congratulations! Picking up a guidebook on writing—whether it's mine or someone else's—shows your commitment to improving your craft. Writing requires a spark of talent, yes, but it's also a skill, or better yet, a profession, that you must learn to master. There are techniques that beginners often don't know, but these techniques can be the difference between a captivating story and a forgettable one. To use a dramatic comparison: no surgeon performs an appendectomy on their first day. They study, train, and practice until they can operate with skill and confidence.

Many of you probably dream of hitting it big with your first publication, creating a bestseller right out of the gate. That's absolutely possible! I know because it happened to me. But here's the truth: before that breakthrough, I spent years writing, rewriting, and devouring every resource on the craft I could find. I attended countless workshops and wrote three entire novels that were never published. Those early projects weren't failures—they were lessons. Each one taught me something invaluable about storytelling.

Eventually, I reached a point where my writing style was polished enough to be both entertaining and marketable. When I finally published my first book, I was rewarded with a rapidly growing fan base. Today, I write fantasy and romance novels for young adults, teach workshops, and offer one-on-one coaching for aspiring writers. Creating this guide felt like the next logical step.

So, without further ado... let's get started!

THE PERFECT BEGINNING

A well-told story doesn't always start at the beginning. In fact, beginning with a lengthy introduction is often a mistake. Avoid drawn-out descriptions of the landscape or overly elaborate attempts to set the mood. Instead, dive straight into the action. The faster your story begins, the easier it is to captivate your reader.

Fast-forward your narrative to the moment when the first significant event occurs. Close your eyes and imagine the scene: what's happening, and where does the tension peak? That's your entry point.

It doesn't matter if the reader doesn't yet know who the characters are or where they are. Those details will unfold naturally as the story progresses. Your primary goal is to hook your audience immediately. This starts with an engaging first paragraph—or better yet, an irresistible first line. A snappy dialogue exchange can work wonders. If your character is alone, create tension through their internal thoughts. Another effective technique is to summarize the core theme of your book in a single, striking sentence—one that hints at the journey ahead. Make it intriguing, but stay true to your genre.

If your opening scene is packed with action, reveal the details gradually. Immerse the reader in the moment as though they've been shoved through a door into the middle of the scene. Skip the formalities of describing the weather or setting up the coat rack. Instead, throw them directly into the action: no backstory, no exposition, no preamble. Let each sentence build upon the last, pulling your audience deeper into the unfolding events.

A compelling opening doesn't just set the stage—it demands attention and promises the reader that they're in for something unforgettable.

CHARACTER DEVELOPMENT

A book lives through its characters. The more three-dimensional they are, the more engaging they become for your readers. Aim to make your characters leap off the page, so by the end of the story, readers feel like they've known them their whole lives.

Breathe life into your characters through movement. If they remain static or motionless, they risk coming across as lifeless cardboard cutouts. Small actions and subtle changes in facial expressions make them more vivid. These gestures create the sense that the reader is in the same room, observing them firsthand. You can also use specific actions to convey emotions without explicitly labeling them.

Consider these small, everyday gestures:

- Scratching their nose
- Running a hand through their hair
- Shifting weight from one foot to the other
- Digging a hole in the ground with the toe of their shoe
- Curling or pressing their lips together
- Crossing their arms
- Wiggling their eyebrows
- Pulling out a pack of gum or mints
- Whistling through their teeth
- Wiping their nose with the back of their hand
- Massaging their temples
- Throwing their hands in the air
- Playing with objects on a table
- And many more.

To write or describe facial expressions more effectively, try standing in front of a mirror. Mimic the expressions your character might make, then describe them as realistically as possible.

There's a golden rule for introducing new characters:

When starting a book, include at least six personal details about your main character within the first two pages. These can be anything—from their favorite toothpaste to their shoe size or preferred TV show. The more details you include, the clearer the image in the reader's mind, helping them relate to the character and connect more easily.

The same principle applies to any significant character introduced later, but not to minor figures like doormen, mail carriers, or sales clerks. Important characters must come to life quickly, as readers want to learn as much as possible about them in a short span.

Key details to include are age, hair color, physique, and clothing. It's frustrating for readers to imagine a heroine with short black hair for three chapters, only to discover she actually has wild red curls. Establish these basics early on, along with the setting and time of year or day.

However, don't simply list these attributes. Instead, weave them naturally into the narrative. When describing outward appearances, add context that shows how these details affect the character. This approach avoids the dreaded 'info-dump' (a clunky, overly direct delivery of information) and instead fosters organic character development.

It's often helpful to create a character sheet for each individual, noting key traits like hair and eye color, stature, age, preferences, and even family history. With a large cast, these details are easy to forget, and searching through the manuscript repeatedly can be tedious.

POV

POV, or *Point of View*, refers to the narrative perspective.

Decide which perspective suits your story best. Will you write in the first person, as though the narrator is speaking directly (I), or in the third person, describing events about 'he' or 'she'?

For the market, both perspectives are equally viable. There will always be readers who prefer one over the other, so choose the one that feels most comfortable for you. That said, first-person perspective is increasingly common in young adult and romance novels. Its diary-like intimacy draws readers deeper into the story, making the experience feel more immediate and personal.

Regardless of your choice, one crucial rule applies: Stay within the narrator's sensory range. Only describe what your narrating character can perceive at that moment.

For instance, if your protagonist is standing with their back to a door and someone enters, they can't know who it is without hearing or seeing a clue.

Wrong: The door opens behind me, and Amy walks in.

Right: I hear the door open behind me, followed by soft footsteps. At the sound of a familiar 'hello', I recognize Amy's voice without turning around.

The same principle applies to unseen events, such as objects falling over behind the character or cars passing by outside their line of sight. Stick to what the character can realistically see, hear, smell, or feel. Anything beyond that ventures into Omni-POV (omniscient point of view), where the narrator knows everything. While Omni-POV has its uses, it creates distance between the reader and the character, often diminishing immersion.

If your story alternates between multiple perspectives, ensure each shift is clear. Start a new chapter for each POV, or use a scene break symbol like *** within chapters.

Avoid 'head-hopping' at all costs. This mistake—switching between perspectives within a single scene without warning—is confusing and disrupts the reader's experience. Clear POV boundaries keep your narrative cohesive and engaging.

SHOW, DON'T TELL!

Becoming an author isn't just about coming up with a good story; it's about telling it in an engaging and vivid way.

The principle of 'SHOW, don't TELL' is one of the most important aspects of writing, though it can be tricky for beginners to master. It essentially means: show actions and details instead of summarizing events.

Here's the key difference:

TELL is used for brief summaries or when conveying information quickly. It provides the necessary facts but doesn't create a vivid mental image. The reader knows what happened but lacks a sense of what the scene looked, felt, smelled, or sounded like.

SHOW allows the author to paint a concrete picture in the reader's mind. Done effectively, it turns the story into a 'mental movie,' immersing the reader completely. This is the true art of storytelling.

To 'show,' rely on strong, specific verbs and avoid overusing adverbs.

Instead of: He went out angrily.

Try: He stomped out. / He thumped the door open and stormed outside.

Instead of: She said grumpily.

Try: She grumbled. / She muttered under her breath.

The goal is to express emotions (hunger, sadness, joy, love, offense, etc.) and states of being through facial expressions, gestures, actions, thoughts, and dialogue—without explicitly naming the emotion.

Example 1

Tell: My sister was ill that morning.

Show: When I stepped into my little sister's room that morning, the sharp scent of cough syrup hit me. On her bedside table, the tongue depressor left by the doctor lay next to a crumpled packet of fever tablets. Sarah sat propped up against her pillows, blowing her nose into a tissue before crumpling it and tossing it into the overflowing trash can. Her red, swollen nose stood out against her pale face, and her watery eyes blinked blearily. The toes of her yellow knitted socks peeked out from beneath the comforter. 'Mom said to bring you a glass of water,' I muttered, tugging my sweater collar up over my nose to block the germs.

Example 2

Tell: After the argument with his ex-girlfriend, he got into his car and drove off in a rage.

Show: 'Damn bitch!' he shouted as she spun on the spiked heels of her boots and stalked off like a runway model. With a sharp tug, he yanked open the door of his black Toyota and threw himself into the driver's seat, growling under his breath. What had he been thinking, coming here again? He knew her too well by now and should have stayed away.

'Damn it!' he snarled, slamming his fist against the steering wheel so hard the speedometer needle jumped behind the glass. His hands trembled as he jammed the key into the ignition, the engine roaring to life with one turn. Tires screeched as he floored the gas pedal, the car lurching forward and leaving a trail of burnt rubber smoke behind. He didn't care who heard the racket or saw him speed down the block at three times the limit.

DILAOGUE

The right dialogue is essential for every genre—horror, historical fiction, comedy, and romance alike. It can add flair and personality to your book or make it feel superficial and dull.

What your characters say—or don't say—matters immensely.

To be effective, dialogue should always fulfill at least one of these purposes:

- Drive the plot forward
- Define characters
- Make a point

Sounds simple, doesn't it? With a little practice, it can be. However, many beginners fall into a common trap: incorporating empty chatter. For instance, having Harald ask his sister about the weather adds no value to the story. Avoid conversations that go nowhere. Every line of dialogue, no matter how brief, should have a deeper meaning. Dialogue should evoke an emotional impact or reveal something significant. Shallow party small talk has no place in your novel.

Natural, but not too realistic

Dialogue must sound natural but shouldn't mirror real-life speech verbatim. In everyday conversation, people often ramble or repeat themselves, but excessive realism in writing can frustrate readers. For example:

'Oh my God, he's coming to the party too?! What am I going to wear? OMG, I really need a new dress! I can't wear something he's seen me in before. Oh my God, oh my God, oh my God!'

While this might reflect actual speech, it's tedious in a novel. After the third 'Oh my God,' your readers may start to skim. Aim for balance: keep dialogue authentic yet concise. Reserve dramatic phrases or expletives for moments of genuine tension or emotional weight, and use repetition sparingly and purposefully.

Adding depth to dialogue

Well-crafted dialogue goes beyond the basics. It can reveal or disguise a character's motivation, hint at future events, or reflect conflict.

Motivation: Use carefully chosen words to show what's driving a character in a particular situation. What's going through their mind? What hidden motives might they have? Avoid being too obvious; instead, rely on subtle paraphrases and allusions.

Foreshadowing: Clever dialogue can build anticipation. Briefly hint at what's at stake without revealing too much. This keeps readers intrigued until the eventual payoff delivers a satisfying 'aha' moment.

Conflict: Conflict is the lifeblood of your story. Use dialogue to heighten tension, reveal emotions, or hint at unspoken disputes. Whether you're writing a romance or a thriller, this adds richness and intensity.

Dialogue pitfalls to avoid

Stiff or overly formal dialogue:

Read your lines aloud. If they sound unnatural or exaggerated, rewrite them. People rarely use perfect grammar in casual speech. Feel free to incorporate slang, abbreviate sentences, or even invent unique phrases.

Stiff: 'Are you okay, my friend?'
Natural: 'You okay, bro?'

Homogeneous voices:

No two individuals speak the same way. However, as the writer, you're responsible for crafting all the dialogue, which can sometimes lead to every character sounding alike. To avoid this, immerse yourself in your characters' personalities. Give each one unique speech patterns. For instance, one character might always address friends by their last names, while another uses nicknames exclusively. Additionally, men often speak in shorter sentences, swear more frequently, and avoid discussing feelings, whereas women may express themselves more elaborately. If a character has a favorite word or phrase, make it uniquely theirs. Nothing is more monotonous than the hero and heroine swearing in the same goddamn way.

By mastering these techniques, your dialogue will not only feel authentic but also drive your story forward in meaningful ways.

Overusing names in dialogue:

Avoid repeatedly using characters' names in conversation. For example:

'Where are you, Laura?' 'I'll be right there, Stefan.' 'Come on now, Laura.'

The actions of your characters and the context of the scene should make it clear who is speaking. Use names sparingly and only to create emotional emphasis or clarify the focus of the conversation.

Actions define dialogue

Strong actions can eliminate the need for repetitive dialogue tags like 'he said' or 'she said.' If you effectively integrate actions into your scenes, the reader will naturally understand who is speaking. For instance:

'I don't believe this,' she said.

Could be replaced with:

She slammed the book shut. 'I don't believe this.'

Avoid writing more than three uninterrupted lines of dialogue without interspersing actions or descriptions. This keeps the reader grounded in the scene, giving them a sense of where the characters are, their physicality, and their mood.

Formatting dialogue

Proper formatting ensures clarity. When a character speaks, their dialogue should appear in its own paragraph. Even if the dialogue is briefly interrupted by an action, keep it within the same paragraph. Start a new paragraph whenever a different character begins speaking. Never combine the dialogue of two or more characters in a single paragraph, as this leads to confusion.

By following these guidelines, your dialogue will not only feel natural and dynamic but will also enhance the depth and flow of your story.

Techniques to spice up your characters' conversations

Sarcasm

Sarcasm is an elegant way to insult someone—when it fits your character's personality. For instance, the Queen of England might not employ sarcasm, but a clever antagonist might wield it like a weapon.

Example:
TONY: Liza and soccer? You might as well try to teach an elephant to dance.
CHLOE: The elephant is spot on.
LIZA (to Chloe): I tried throwing up my food once in ninth grade, but that's probably more your thing.

Sarcasm isn't easy to write and doesn't suit every character. It's more of an inherent trait than something learned. If sarcasm doesn't come naturally to you, don't force it—readers will notice.

Quick-wittedness

A snappy retort or witty comeback can elevate dialogue. Typically, the first line is strong, but the response should surpass it in cleverness.

Example (from *Gilmore Girls – a phone call*):
LORELAI: That dress is too slutty!
MOTHER: Not the dress, but the woman wearing it...
LORELAI: Oh, the connection's broken—the house is going through a tunnel!

Double entendre

Double entendre involves creating a line with two distinct meanings, often layering a pun or playful ambiguity over a statement. This technique works well in lighter, more playful scenes or to add subtle humor.

Example (from *The Silence of the Lambs*):
HANNIBAL LECTER: I do wish we could chat longer, but... I'm having an old friend for dinner.

Double entendre can create intrigue and depth, especially when it fits the tone and context of the scene. By using this technique, you engage the reader's imagination and add a clever edge to your dialogue.

Exaggeration and understatement

Use irony to either blow a situation out of proportion or play it down. For instance, 'Houston, we have a problem' is a masterful understatement that carries significant weight.

By mastering these techniques, you can craft dynamic and memorable dialogue that enhances your characters and story.

Conflict

Conflict is the heartbeat of any story. Without it, a narrative risks becoming a dull sequence of 'nice' scenes that neither challenge the characters nor grip the reader.

But what exactly is conflict?

At its core, conflict occurs when the goals, values, or desires of individuals or groups collide, creating tension and driving the story forward. It can be as simple as a character debating a personal decision or as grand as an epic battle between good and evil.

In fiction, conflict typically falls into two categories:

Internal Conflict: A character's inner struggle—facing fears, flaws, or moral dilemmas.

External Conflict: Obstacles that arise from forces outside the character—antagonists, societal pressures, or physical challenges.

Internal Conflict:

This is where the soul of your story resides. Internal conflict allows readers to connect deeply with your characters as they wrestle with personal demons or evolve emotionally. Think of Ebenezer Scrooge in *A Christmas Carol*: his journey isn't about fighting villains or saving the world—it's about saving himself. His transformation from a cold-hearted miser to a compassionate man is what makes his story timeless and touching.

External Conflict:

External conflict adds excitement and stakes to a story. It's what makes readers sit on the edge of their seats. Consider *Harry Potter*: Harry's journey is filled with perilous adventures, from battling dark wizards to protecting his friends. But while the plot revolves around these external challenges, it's Harry's emotional growth—his courage, loyalty, and resilience—that makes the story unforgettable. External conflicts often create opportunities for internal growth, adding depth to the character and story.

Every great story follows a conflict arc:

1. **Introduction of the Conflict**: The characters discover what's at stake.
2. **Rising Action**: Tension builds as they face obstacles and setbacks.
3. **Climax**: The ultimate showdown where everything hangs in the balance.

4. **Resolution**: Loose ends are tied up, and the characters emerge changed.

Readers experience this arc emotionally. They should feel the rising tension, the heart-pounding climax, and the cathartic release of resolution. Without conflict, the reader has no reason to care, no rollercoaster of emotions to ride.

If your story lacks conflict, it lacks purpose. Ask yourself: What's at stake? What will keep readers turning the pages? If you can't answer these questions, it's time to revisit your plot.

PLOT

Plotting is where your story takes shape—a creative dance between imagination and structure. Think of it as the blueprint for your novel. Whether you meticulously outline every chapter or prefer to dive in headfirst and let the story unfold, plotting gives your narrative direction.

Some writers approach plotting like architects, carefully crafting detailed outlines. Others are more like explorers, setting off without a map and discovering the story as they go. Both approaches are valid, and there's no 'right' way to plot—only the way that works best for you.

Tips for Plotting:

Outline or bullet points: Create a roadmap for your story. List key events or chapter summaries to keep you on track.

Leave room for flexibility: Characters often take on lives of their own, steering the plot in unexpected directions. Embrace this—it's a sign that your story is alive and dynamic.

Here's a secret: No matter how carefully you plot, your story will likely evolve!

Characters might speak or act in ways you didn't anticipate. A subplot you thought was minor could grow into a major turning point. This unpredictability isn't a failure—it's magic.

For example, imagine you've planned a story about a shy protagonist finding love. But as you write, you realize their journey is less about romance and more about self-discovery. Follow that instinct. It often leads to richer, more authentic stories.

If you ever feel stuck in the story, return to your plot. Is the conflict strong enough? Do the stakes feel real? Sometimes, tweaking the plot can reignite your creativity.

Remember, the end result doesn't have to perfectly match your initial plan. Some of the greatest stories surprise even their creators. Let the process guide you, and trust that your story knows where it's going.

Prologue and Epilogue

A common question in my workshops is: *Should I include a prologue or epilogue? Are readers expecting one?*

Prologue

A prologue can be useful when your readers need important background information—something that happened in your characters' past and is vital to understanding the story. This information might not fit seamlessly into the main narrative and could instead disrupt its flow if introduced later through flashbacks.

Why not use flashbacks?

While flashbacks can be effective, they often come with a significant drawback: they interrupt the momentum of the story. Imagine you've skillfully drawn your readers into the narrative, and they're fully immersed in the current events. A sudden flashback jolts them out of the present, forcing them to adjust to a different timeline. By the time they reorient themselves, they're pulled back into the present, disrupting their reading flow twice in quick succession.

This becomes particularly problematic if multiple flashbacks occur throughout the book, fragmenting the narrative further. Instead, a well-crafted prologue can summarize critical past events, allowing you to establish essential context without breaking the story's rhythm later.

Tips for writing an effective prologue:

Keep it relevant: Only include events that are essential to understanding your story. Avoid unnecessary details that bog down the reader.

End on a hook: Conclude the prologue at a suspenseful or intriguing moment. This keeps readers curious, setting up an 'aha' moment later when the story ties back to it.

Avoid overloading: Your prologue shouldn't reveal everything. Leave some mysteries unresolved for the main narrative.

Length matters: Aim for 2–10 book pages. Keep it shorter than or equal to the length of your regular chapters.

Finally, treat your prologue with the same care as the rest of your story. Introduce characters vividly, make them feel real, and *show* the events unfolding rather than simply summarizing them.

Epilogue

In my experience as a romance author, the epilogue serves as a delightful bonus. While not strictly necessary, it's an excellent opportunity to leave your readers with a sense of closure and satisfaction.

Think of it this way: After spending days or even weeks immersed in your story, laughing, crying, and rooting for your characters, readers often aren't ready to let go. The epilogue offers a gentle descent from the emotional highs of the climax, allowing them to savor a final moment with the characters they've come to love. It's the cherry on top of an already delicious sundae—the story is complete without it, but it's just that much sweeter with it.

Why include an epilogue?

Closure: Tie up loose ends or answer lingering questions.

A glimpse into the future: Show what happens to your characters beyond the final chapter. Did they live happily ever after? Did they achieve their dreams?

Reader delight: Provide a sense of reward for readers who have invested their time and emotions in your story.

Unlike the prologue, the length of the epilogue is flexible. It can be as short as a page or as long as a full chapter. Some authors even use the epilogue to hint at future storylines or sequels, though this depends on your genre and writing style.

The prologue and epilogue are tools, not rules. Use them only if they enhance your story. If a prologue provides clarity or intrigue, and an epilogue offers closure or joy, they can elevate your novel. However, if they feel forced or unnecessary, it's better to leave them out. Ultimately, your goal is to give readers an experience they'll cherish—one that lingers long after they've turned the final page.

ORDER OF CHAPTERS

How should you approach writing a book? Should you write each chapter sequentially, as they appear in the final version, or can you jump ahead and write later chapters first, then slot them in later?

Here's my clear and emphatic advice: Stay in line!

Your characters—and your story—will evolve naturally as the conflict unfolds. The person your character is in Chapter 17 will be vastly different from the person they were in Chapter 3. Their emotions, thoughts, and even their core motivations will shift as they face challenges and grow. This evolution affects not only your characters but also the overall tone and energy of the story.

Why writing out of order is problematic:

At first, jumping ahead may seem like a great idea. You have a burst of inspiration for a scene in Chapter 17, so you write it down. The characters' actions and emotions feel perfectly consistent, and the words flow effortlessly. You think, *This is gold—I'll just slot this in later.*

But as you continue writing chapters 13 through 16, you'll notice something: that 'perfect' chapter no longer fits.

Why?

Character development: By the time you reach Chapter 17, your characters will have gone through experiences and changes you couldn't fully anticipate when you skipped ahead. Their emotions, decisions, and perspectives will no longer align with what you wrote earlier.

Subtle details: Along the way, you'll have added layers of depth—small details, subplots, or emotional nuances—that didn't exist when you originally wrote the later chapter. These omissions create gaps in logic or tone that can't easily be patched.

Flow disruption: The transition from Chapter 16 to your prewritten Chapter 17 might feel jarring. Even with extensive revisions, the earlier writing may lack the seamless continuity required to keep readers immersed in the story.

What initially seemed like a shortcut ends up feeling like a stumbling block, throwing off the pacing and emotional resonance of your book.

A better approach:

To save yourself time and frustration, resist the temptation to write chapters out of order. Instead, take extensive notes on the ideas you're eager to include later. For example:

Dialogue: If you have a specific conversation in mind, jot it down in a separate document.

Scenes or concepts: Outline the general action, emotions, and themes you want to explore, leaving room for adjustments based on the story's progression.

Characters: Note how you imagine the characters will feel or act in that moment, but remain flexible—future chapters may evolve in unexpected ways.

By doing this, you preserve your inspiration without locking yourself into a version of events that may no longer align with your story later.

The payoff of writing chronologically:

When you write chapters in order, you stay in tune with the 'vibe' of the book. Each chapter flows naturally from the one before, maintaining consistency in tone, pacing, and character development. If you reach Chapter 17 and still want to include elements from your earlier notes, you can incorporate them organically—tailored to the mood and energy of the story at that moment.

Yes, this approach may seem slower at first, but it saves you the painstaking work of retrofitting scenes, rewriting entire sections, or losing that smooth narrative flow your readers crave.

Remember, writing a novel is like taking a journey—you can't skip ahead to the destination without first walking the path that gets you there.

FORMATING

How should you format your book? There are two main formats to consider:

Working Format: Used throughout the writing process to keep your manuscript clear, organized, and easy to edit.

Publishing Format: Prepared when your book is ready for upload to Amazon or other sales platforms.

Working Format

During the writing process, clarity and readability are your top priorities. Use the following settings for your manuscript:

- **Text alignment**: Justified (flush left and right).
- **Paragraph indentation**: First line of each paragraph indented by 0.5 inches.
- **Font**: Times New Roman.
- **Font size**: 12 point.
- **Line spacing**: Double.
- **Page numbers**: Positioned at the bottom of each page.
- **Chapter headings**: Use Word's 'Heading 1' style. Customize the appearance of your headings through the 'Modify' option in the Styles menu. This will also make it easier to generate a table of contents later.

Why double line spacing?

Double spacing improves readability, allows you to spot mistakes more easily, and makes specific passages easier to locate during editing.

Keep paragraphs short.

Paragraphs that are too long can feel overwhelming. Instead, aim for concise paragraphs of 2–5 sentences. Think of a line break as matching a natural pause or deep breath. Shorter paragraphs keep the reader engaged and improve the overall flow.

Publishing Format

When your manuscript is finalized, you'll need to make a few adjustments to prepare it for upload:

- **Change line spacing:** Switch from double spacing to single spacing.
- **Adjust chapter openings:** Remove the indent on the first line of each chapter. Only the very first line of each chapter should align flush left; the rest of the paragraphs should retain their indents.
- **Add front and back matter**

Front Matter:

Title page with the book title and author name.

Copyright page with publication details and disclaimers.

Table of contents (use Word's table of contents generator).

Back Matter:

A preview of your next book (optional).

A list of your other works.

A short author bio.

Final Cleanup

Before uploading your manuscript, perform these final steps to eliminate formatting errors:

Step 1: Remove Double Spaces

1. Open Word's **Search and Replace** tool.
2. In the 'Find' field, enter two spaces.
3. In the 'Replace' field, enter one space.

4. Click 'Replace All' and repeat until Word reports 0 changes.

Step 2: Remove Spaces Before Paragraphs

1. Open **Search and Replace** again.
2. In the 'Find' field, enter: ^p

(This searches for a paragraph mark followed by a space.)

3. In the 'Replace' field, enter: ^p

(This removes the space after the paragraph mark.)

4. Click 'Replace All' and repeat until Word reports 0 changes.

Step 3: Remove Spaces After Paragraphs

1. Open **Search and Replace** again.
2. In the 'Find' field, enter: ^p

(This searches for a space followed by a paragraph mark.)

3. In the 'Replace' field, enter: ^p
(This removes the space before the paragraph mark.)
4. Click 'Replace All' and repeat until Word reports 0 changes.

Your script is ready!

Once your manuscript is properly formatted and thoroughly proofread, it's ready to upload. Whether you're publishing on Amazon or another platform, these steps ensure a professional-looking book that meets industry standards.

BLURB

For many authors, writing a blurb can feel like a daunting task—but it doesn't have to be. Think of it as an exciting challenge: the chance to distill your story into a few tantalizing lines that captivate potential readers.

A great blurb briefly summarizes the first 3 to 5 chapters of your book and ends with a compelling hook—a final line that creates suspense and leaves readers eager to dive in.

Key elements of a blurb

Your blurb should include:

The Protagonists: Name and age to help readers quickly connect with your characters.

The Theme: What is the central idea or emotional core of the story?

A Surprising Twist: A hint at a key event or challenge that disrupts the status quo.

The Hook: A final, unforgettable line that piques curiosity and compels readers to open the book.

What a blurb is (and isn't):

A blurb is not a complete summary of your book. Instead, it's a teaser—a way to intrigue readers and encourage them to read the sample chapters. Most samples consist of the first one or two chapters, so your blurb should focus on enticing them into that initial part of the story.

Keep it short and powerful:

The shorter and more concise your blurb, the better. Readers browsing through dozens of books don't have time to read lengthy descriptions. A strong blurb, often just four or five sentences, can stand out and hold their attention.

Here are some tips:

Reflect the Voice of Your Book: If your novel is lighthearted, let the tone of the blurb reflect that. If it's dark and suspenseful, the language should match.

Avoid Bullet Points: Your blurb should feel fluid and compelling, not like a checklist.

Build Tension: Use dynamic, genre-specific language to excite your readers and leave them wanting more.

The Hook: Your blurb's secret weapon

The hook is the single most important element of your blurb. It's what stays with readers and nudges them to hit 'buy.' Unfortunately, many authors make the mistake of ending their blurbs with predictable yes-or-no questions.

Example of a weak hook:

'Will Sarah manage to overcome her prejudices and fall in love?'

Problem: The answer is obvious. Readers don't need to read the book to guess what happens.
Instead, craft a hook that sparks curiosity and cannot be easily answered. Use open-ended questions like 'How,' 'Who,' or 'What.' Or create a sharp, provocative statement that leaves readers wanting more.

Examples of Effective Hooks

1. A question that intrigues
'How will Sarah handle her growing feelings when the truth about his past threatens to destroy everything she's built?'

2. A statement that stirs emotion

'She thought she was safe—until the man she trusted most became the one person she couldn't escape.'

Writing a great blurb takes practice, but don't let it intimidate you. Focus on creating a mini-story that excites readers and gives them just enough to make them curious. Keep it short, hook them with suspense, and let the voice of your book shine through.

Above all, remember this: Your blurb is the first handshake between your story and your readers. Make it firm, memorable, and impossible to resist.

CRITIQUE

As much as we value the opinions of friends and family, they are not ideal critique partners. Their love for you often prevents them from providing honest feedback. Instead, seek critique from professional writers—people who understand the craft and know what to look for in a manuscript.

Critique comes with rules!

Writing is a craft, and like any profession, it has rules that must be learned. Talent is important, but it's not enough on its own.

Receiving your first professional critique can be overwhelming. Be prepared for shock and even tears—it's part of the process. A thorough critique will likely reveal that your manuscript is far from perfect. It may need deep revisions, possibly several rounds, before it's ready for publication.

Here's how to handle a critique:

Read it through: Go over the feedback carefully.
Take a break: Step away for a few hours or days. Allow yourself to process the emotional sting before returning to it.
Revisit with fresh eyes: Once the initial shock wears off, revisit the critique with an open mind and start analyzing the suggestions.
Remember: Critique is not personal. It targets your writing, not you. Most critiques focus on writing technique and story structure, with the goal of helping you improve.

Harsh feedback is a gift!

Sometimes critiques are blunt, and that's okay. If someone points out a recurring issue, it's because they want to help you grow as a writer. Take time to consider every suggestion, but remember: you are the master of your book!

You don't have to accept every piece of feedback. If something feels wrong or doesn't align with your vision, trust your instincts. Your writing should remain true to your voice. See critiques as a toolkit to refine your work—not a prescription to rewrite it in someone else's style.

Critique partners

The ideal critique partner:

- Is a writer, preferably in the same genre.
- Is as skilled as you—or better.
- Respects your voice and style.
- Prioritizes professionalism over friendship.

How to find a critique partner:

- Join author groups on Facebook or other writing communities.
- Start your own critique group, exchanging chapters for feedback.
- Do a trial swap of a chapter or two to see if you're compatible.

Finding the perfect critique partner is like finding the perfect life partner—it requires patience, compromise, and trust. When you find someone who challenges you constructively and helps you grow, they're worth their weight in gold.

Why you need a critique partner

Even the most experienced authors benefit from fresh eyes. As the creator, you know your story too well to spot gaps or weaknesses. A critique partner offers an outsider's perspective, showing you what works and what doesn't.

Critique partners cost nothing but time, and the rewards are invaluable. Plus, they'll celebrate your successes with you—and a little praise can do wonders for the writer's soul.

Writer's Block

It happens to everyone.

Writer's block can strike at any time, and there's no universal cure. The key is understanding what triggered it and finding your way through it.

Shake off the pressure!

Often, writer's block stems from stress or self-imposed pressure. When this happens, step away from your manuscript and focus on something completely different. Here are some ideas:

- Go shopping.
- Redesign your writing space.
- Clean the house.
- Spend time with friends.
- Work on marketing for another book.

The goal is to *let go*. Writing under tension rarely produces your best work.

Trust the process!

Writing is a deeply ingrained part of who you are. If it's in your blood, it will come back when the time is right. In the meantime, focus on enjoying the present moment.

Remember: Writer's block isn't the end of your creativity—it's just a pause. Allow yourself to rest, recharge, and return to writing when inspiration strikes.

Correction

When polishing your manuscript, two essential services come into play: **editing** and **proofreading.**

Editing

If you're a beginner without an experienced critique partner (a fellow author who helps refine your manuscript during the writing process), hiring a professional editor is crucial. An editor reviews your manuscript for:

Plot Issues: Identifying inconsistencies or pacing problems.
Style: Improving flow and tone.
Dialogue: Ensuring it's natural and fits the characters.

'Show vs. Tell': Highlighting areas where you can replace flat exposition with vivid, immersive descriptions.

Editing is thorough and transformative, addressing the deeper mechanics of storytelling. While it costs between $3.50 and $6.50 per standard page, it's a necessary investment if you aim to become a professional author. Remember, a poorly edited manuscript can tarnish your reputation, especially as a self-publisher, where first impressions are everything.

Proofreading

Proofreading focuses solely on correcting spelling, grammar, and punctuation errors. It's typically less expensive than editing, with costs ranging from $2.50 to $4.50 per standard page.
AI may do the job as well.

Before you choose an editor or proofreader:

- **negotiate, but don't compromise quality**: It's okay to ask for a discount, but don't base your decision solely on price.
- **check qualifications**: Ensure the editor or proofreader has a relevant degree (e.g., in languages, literature, or linguistics).
- **request samples**: Ask for 3–5 standard pages of edited text to assess their skills. Send them raw, unpolished material so you can see their true abilities.
- **compare samples**: Review all returned samples and choose the editor whose work resonates with you. Trust your instincts, not just the price tag.
- **don't forget the blurb:** Your blurb is just as important as the manuscript itself. Make sure it gets the same level of professional attention before publication.

PITCH

Pitching is the art of presenting your manuscript to a publisher or literary agency. It's your chance to make a great first impression, so every detail counts.

How to craft a successful pitch

Personalized Greeting: Address the recipient by name.

Tailored introduction: Explain why you're pitching to this specific publisher or agency. Mention what you admire about their work, their authors, or their focus.

Professional tone: Keep the letter polished and professional. Injecting a bit of your personality is fine, but avoid being overly casual.

Brief overview: Summarize your book in one or two sentences, but save the detailed description for the synopsis.

Transparency: If you're pitching to multiple agencies, it's acceptable to mention this. However, avoid listing names of agencies that have already rejected you.

Proofread before sending: Errors in your pitch can ruin an otherwise excellent submission. Make sure your letter is flawless.

Track your submissions: Keep a detailed list of where and when you've pitched your manuscript to avoid duplicate emails.

Avoid resubmissions: Once you've sent your pitch, resist the urge to tweak or resend it. Changing your mind post-submission appears unprofessional.

Timing matters!

Avoid pitching right after major industry events like the Leipzig and Frankfurt Book Fairs or during the holiday season. During these times, agents and publishers are often overwhelmed, reducing the likelihood of a thoughtful response.

Pseudonym

A pseudonym is an alternative author name you can use if you prefer not to publish your work under your real name.

Should you use a pseudonym?
The choice of whether to use a pseudonym depends entirely on your preferences and circumstances.

Stick to Your Real Name: If you're proud of your name and want to openly associate yourself with your work, there's no need for a pseudonym.

Choose a Pseudonym: If you're writing in a genre like erotica or another niche that might make you uncomfortable being associated with your work publicly, a pseudonym can offer privacy and peace of mind.

Of course, you can also adopt a pseudonym simply because you like the idea or feel it suits your creative identity better. Whatever your reason, there are a few important considerations when choosing one.

How to choose the right pseudonym

Pick a name you connect with

Choose a pseudonym that feels authentic to you—one you can identify with over the long term. The closer it is to your real name or something meaningful to you, the easier it will feel to embrace. Names that initially seem exciting can become less appealing after repeated use, so take your time with this decision.

Test your pseudonym

Before committing, create a mock book cover featuring your chosen pseudonym. Use a simple image that resembles a real book cover and place your pseudonym prominently in capital letters at the top or bottom. Save the cover and look at it regularly for a few weeks. If the name still resonates with you after that, it's a good choice. If it doesn't, try a different pseudonym and repeat the process.

A pseudonym is more than just a name—it becomes a part of your author identity. Whether you use one for privacy, branding, or creative expression, take the time to make a thoughtful choice.

Social Media

As an author, three social media components are essential to building your brand and connecting with readers:

- **Your Website**
- **Your Blog**
- **Your Social Media Profiles**

Each serves a unique purpose and, when used effectively, can help you grow your readership and enhance your author presence.

1. The Website

Your website is your home base—a static, professional space where readers can find essential information about you and your books. At a minimum, your website should answer these questions:

Who are you? Share a brief, engaging bio.

What books have you written? Include a complete list, with links for purchase.

How can readers contact you? Provide a contact form or email address.
Once you've covered the basics, consider adding:

FAQ page: Answer common questions about your writing process or books.

Bonus material: Offer extras like deleted scenes, character backstories, or sneak peeks.

News/Updates page: Share announcements about upcoming releases or events.

Blog integration: If you have a blog, include it seamlessly on your site.

Make it appealing: Design your website in a style that reflects your books and brand. Avoid filler text or unnecessary 'blah blah blah.' Every page should have a clear purpose.

Pro tip: Avoid free URLs that include the provider's name (e.g., *suesmith.wordpress.com*). For a professional appearance, invest in a custom domain. Most providers charge between $30 and $50 per year to remove their branding from your URL—it's worth it.

2. The Blog

A blog gives you a dynamic platform to connect with readers and share updates in real-time. Some website providers, like WordPress, include blog functionality; if yours doesn't, consider setting up a separate blog on a platform like Blogspot and link to it from your website.

What to Blog About:

Share what's on your mind.

Announce new projects, releases, or events.

Build anticipation for upcoming books with cover reveals, blurbs, or teasers.

Posting Frequency:

Aim for a new post every 2–4 weeks, but don't force it. Quality trumps quantity.

If you leave a particularly engaging post up for a longer time, that's fine—it keeps readers interested.

Remember: A blog is a tool, not a burden. Post when you have something meaningful to share, not out of obligation.

3. Facebook, Instagram, and TikTok

Social media platforms are your direct connection to readers. Use them to engage your audience, build relationships, and grow your community.

Facebook:

Create an **official author page** separate from your private profile. This page is public and represents your professional presence.

Share updates, engage in discussions, and host giveaways or competitions.

Always maintain a friendly, positive tone. Avoid personal rants, political debates, or negative interactions. If you encounter offensive comments, delete them without engaging.

Instagram and TikTok:

These visually driven platforms are perfect for showcasing your creativity. Share:

Beautiful images of your books or writing space.

Behind-the-scenes glimpses of your writing process.

Short, fun videos to promote your work.

Engagement tips:

Encourage discussions by asking questions or running contests.

Offer variety in giveaways—don't just give signed books but also include themed extras or personal touches.

Keep conditions simple for competitions, especially for new readers. Avoid asking them to purchase your book to participate; instead, use fun, easy tasks to engage them.

Proofread before posting! Mistakes can undermine your professionalism. Read every post carefully before sharing. If you spot an error later, use the edit function to correct it.

Don't let Social Media consume your writing time. While more platforms mean more visibility, managing too many accounts can eat into your creative energy. Prioritize quality over quantity.

The truth about likes:

It's tempting to fixate on the number of likes or followers, but these metrics don't define your success. Instead of chasing numbers, focus on creating meaningful content for your audience.

Never Buy Likes: Purchasing followers undermines your credibility. Readers will notice if you have thousands of followers but no meaningful engagement. Authenticity is far more valuable.

Social media is a powerful tool for connecting with your readers and building your brand. With a professional website, an engaging blog, and an active presence on key platforms like Facebook, Instagram, and TikTok, you can grow your audience while staying true to your creative voice.

Balance is key: Use these tools to enhance your writing career, not distract from it.

Backup

Losing months of work due to a computer failure, theft, or an unforeseen disaster like a house fire is every author's nightmare. To protect yourself from this heartache, it's essential to back up your book files in multiple locations—ideally, two or three times.

Here's a useful backup strategy:

- **Backup on your PC**: Save all files in a dedicated folder on your computer.
- **External hard drive**: Regularly copy your files to an external hard drive for extra security.
- **Offsite backup**: Once a year, I back up my files to an external hard drive stored at my mother's house, 300 km away. This ensures a

safe copy exists even if something happens to my home equipment.

- **Email backup**: Upload your files via email. Save your book files, covers, and other essential materials as email attachments and store them in your drafts or a designated folder. No matter what happens to your hardware, you can always access your email backups from any device.

This simple system can save you immense grief in an emergency.

Pro Tip: If you need to share your manuscript—whether it's a full book, a single chapter, or supplementary materials—always use email instead of messenger apps. Messenger platforms are not secure for this purpose and can lead to data loss or unauthorized access.

Good Luck!

That's it for now! I hope you find these lessons and tips useful as you embark on your writing journey. With practice and persistence, you'll discover that the process isn't as daunting as it might seem.

Above all, don't give up. Keep your goal in mind and take it one step at a time.

Now, I wish you lots of fun, creativity, and success as you write your first bestseller!

BOOKS BY ANNA KATMORE

ON THIN ICE

Counting Fireflies

Splintered North

*

Seventeen Butterflies

GROVER BEACH PLAYERS

Play With Me

Ryan Hunter

T Is For...

Dating Trouble

The Trouble with Dating Sue

FALL FOR ME

The Impossible Bet

This Kitten Has Claws

CRUSHED HEARTS

Unfair Love

Broken Dawn

Awaking Trust

ADVENTURES IN NEVERLAND

Neverland

Pan's Revenge

THE TRUE CHRONICLES OF FAIRYLAND

A Prince for Little Red Riding Hood

A Wolf in her Way

*

Three Shades of Sinful

You were my Fairytale

My Secret Vampire

ELOYN

About the Author

"I'm writing stories because I can't breathe without."

At six years old, Anna Katmore told everyone she wanted to be an author after she discovered her mother's typewriter on a rainy afternoon. She could just see herself typing away on that magical thing for the rest of her life.

In 2012, she finished her first young adult romance "Play With Me" which was the beginning of her true writing career, with many books to follow.

Today, she lives in an enchanted world of her own, where she combines storytelling with teaching, and she never tires of bringing a little bit of magic into the lives of her beloved readers, too.

Anna's favorite quote and something she lives by:
If your dreams don't scare you, they aren't big enough.

For more information, please visit:
www.annakatmore.com

www.ingramcontent.com/pod-product-compliance
Lightning Source LLC
La Vergne TN
LVHW091122150826
845673LV00002B/940